W9-BNS-478

MAY   2008

ORLAND PARK PUBLIC LIBRARY
14921 RAVINIA AVENUE
ORLAND PARK, ILLINOIS 60462
708-428-5100

DEMCO

Pebble Plus

Life around the World

School in Many Cultures

by Heather Adamson

Consulting Editor: Gail Saunders-Smith, PhD

Capstone press

Mankato, Minnesota

ORLAND PARK PUBLIC LIBRARY

e371
ADA

Pebble Plus is published by Capstone Press,
151 Good Counsel Drive, P.O. Box 669, Mankato, Minnesota 56002.
www.capstonepress.com

Copyright © 2008 by Capstone Press, a Coughlan Publishing Company. All rights reserved.
No part of this publication may be reproduced in whole or in part, or stored in a retrieval system, or
transmitted in any form or by any means, electronic, mechanical, photocopying, recording, or otherwise,
without written permission of the publisher. For information regarding permission, write to Capstone Press,
151 Good Counsel Drive, P.O. Box 669, Dept. R, Mankato, Minnesota 56002.
Printed in the United States of America

1 2 3 4 5 6 12 11 10 09 08 07

Library of Congress Cataloging-in-Publication Data
Adamson, Heather, 1974–
    School in many cultures / by Heather Adamson.
    p. cm.— (Pebble plus. Life around the world)
    Summary: "Simple text and photographs present school from many cultures"—Provided by publisher.
    Includes bibliographical references and index.
    ISBN-13: 978-1-4296-0021-7 (hardcover)
    ISBN-10: 1-4296-0021-7 (hardcover)
    1. Schools—Juvenile literature. 2. School children—Juvenile literature. I. Title. II. Series.
    LB1513.A35 2008
    371—dc22   2006101958

Editorial Credits
Sarah L. Schuette, editor; Alison Thiele, set designer; Kara Birr, photo researcher

Photo Credits
Corbis/CORBIS SABA/Ricki Rosen, 7; Michael Prince, cover (India); Paul A. Souders, 17; Star Ledger/
    Vic Yepello, 9
Peter Arnold/Jorgen Schytte, 11, 19; Ron Giling, 21; Sean Sprague, 5, 13
Shutterstock/Fred S., 1 (Canada); Nadejda Ivanova, 15

Note to Parents and Teachers

The Life around the World set supports national social studies standards related to
culture and geography. This book describes and illustrates school in many cultures. The
images support early readers in understanding the text. The repetition of words and
phrases helps early readers learn new words. This book also introduces early readers
to subject-specific vocabulary words, which are defined in the Glossary section. Early
readers may need assistance to read some words and to use the Table of Contents,
Glossary, Read More, Internet Sites, and Index sections of the book.

Table of Contents

Places to Learn

Students go to school

in many cultures.

How is your school

like other schools?

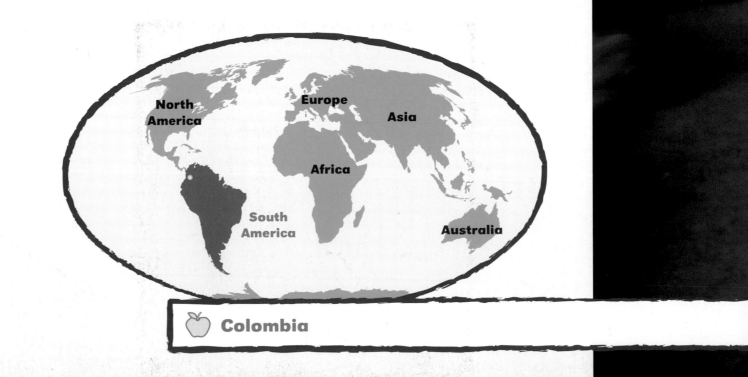

🍎 Colombia

4

Teachers work at school.

They teach many subjects.

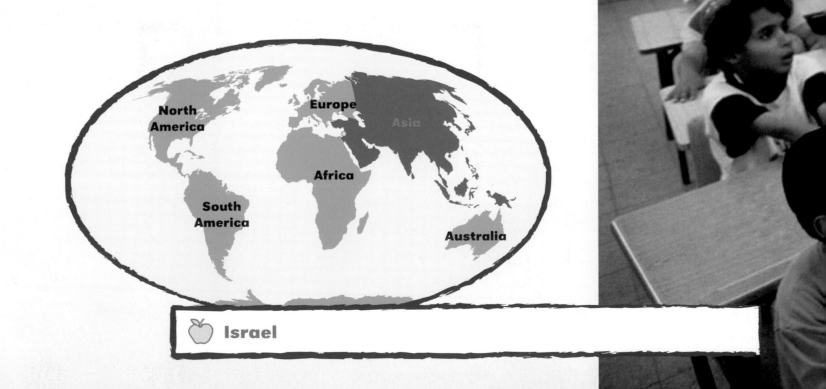

🍎 Israel

In Class

Students learn in classrooms.
A girl in the United States
does math on a chalkboard.

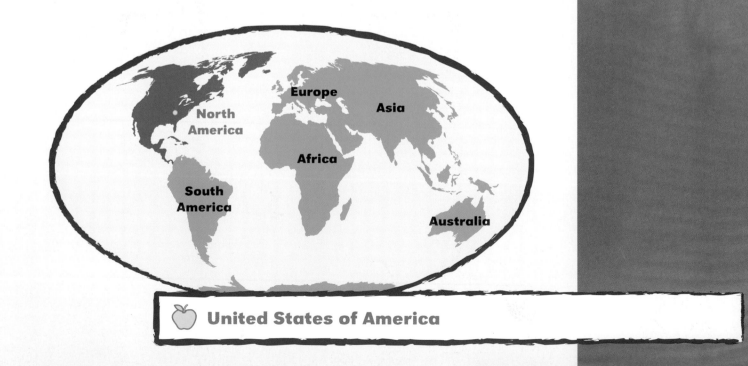

North America

Europe

Asia

Africa

South America

Australia

United States of America

Students learn outside.

A class in Vietnam studies

science and art at a park.

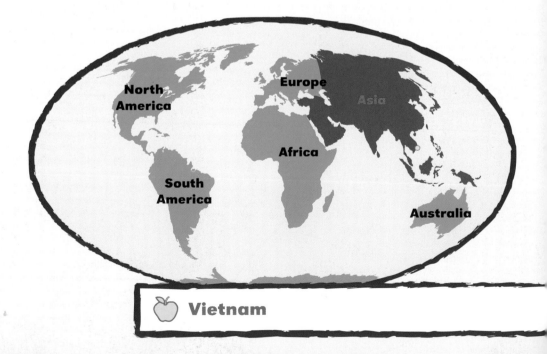

Students take notes.

A boy in Africa

listens to his teacher.

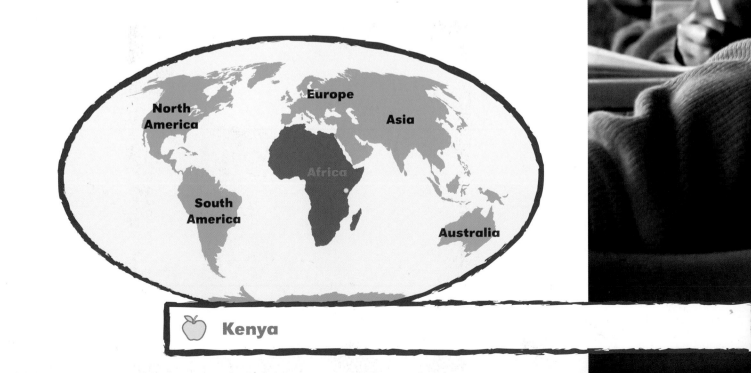

North America

Europe

Asia

Africa

South America

Australia

🍎 Kenya

Fun at School

Students go on field trips.
A class in France learns
about a castle.

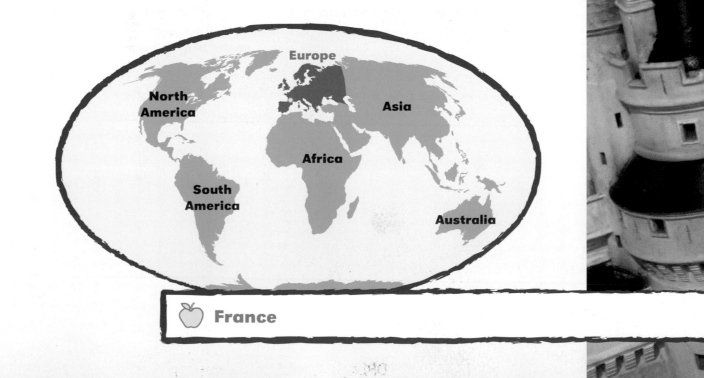

North America

South America

Europe

Africa

Asia

Australia

France

479 5725

15

LAND PARK PUBLIC LIBRARY

Students take lunch breaks.

Friends in Australia

eat together outside.

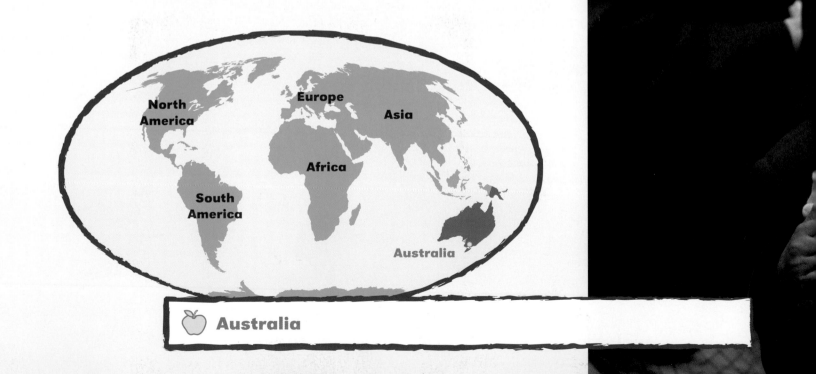

Australia

Students play at recess.

A girl in Africa jumps rope
with her friends.

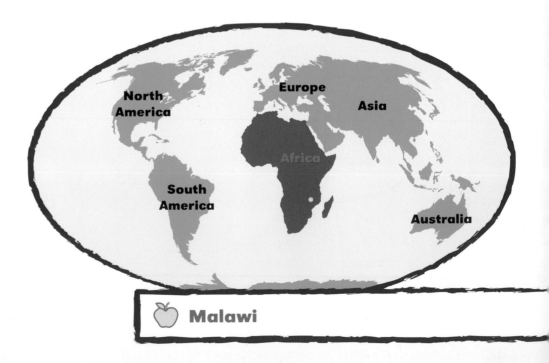

Your School

Around the world, students
laugh and learn at school.
Where do you go to school?

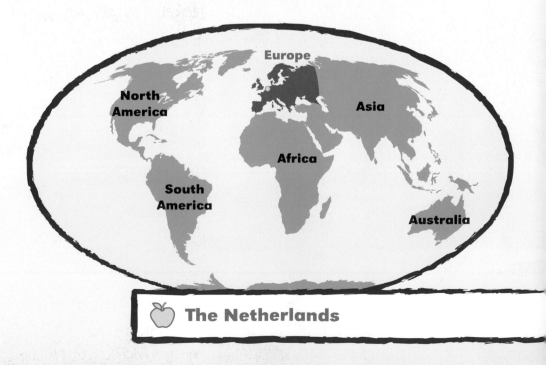

North
America

Europe

Asia

Africa

South
America

Australia

The Netherlands

21

Glossary

classroom—a room in a school where classes are taught; classrooms can be in buildings or places outside where students gather.

culture—the way of life, ideas, customs, and traditions of a group of people

field trip—a trip to see and learn something new; classes often go on field trips to museums, zoos, and other interesting places.

math—the study of numbers, shapes, and measurements and how they relate to each other

science—the study of nature and the world

subject—an area of study; students learn subjects such as math, science, art, and music at school.

Read More

Doering, Amanda. *School ABC: An Alphabet Book.* A+ Books: Alphabet Books. Mankato, Minn.: Capstone Press, 2005.

Miller, Jake. *Who's Who in a School Community.* Communities at Work. New York: PowerKids Press, 2005.

Rayner, Amanda. *Going to School.* One World. North Mankato, Minn.: Smart Apple Media, 2006.

Internet Sites

FactHound offers a safe, fun way to find Internet sites related to this book. All of the sites on FactHound have been researched by our staff.

Here's how

1. Visit *www.facthound.com*

2. Choose your grade level.

3. Type in this book ID **1429600217** for age-appropriate sites. You may also browse subjects by clicking on letters, or by clicking on pictures and words.

4. Click on the **Fetch It** button.

FactHound will fetch the best sites for you!

Index

Word Count: 113
Grade: 1
Early-Intervention Level: 12

ORLAND PARK PUBLIC LIBRARY